Fram

Keith Reddin is a graduate of Northwestern University and the Yale Drama School. His adaptation of Mikhail Shatrov's *Maybe* starred Vanessa Redgrave (Royal Exchange, Manchester, 1993). He adapted Mikhail Bulgakov's *Black Snow* (Goodman Theatre, Chicago 1993) which won the Joseph Jefferson Award for Best Play. He has also written several films including *All The Rage* and *The Heart Of Justice*. Other plays include *Life and Limb, Rum and Coke, Nebraska, Life During Wartime, Brutality of Fact* and *All the Rage*.

Published by Methuen 2002

1 3 5 7 9 10 8 6 4 2

First published in the Great Britain in 2002 by
Methuen Publishing Limited
215 Vauxhall Bridge Road,
London SW1V 1EJ

Copyright © Keith Reddin 2002

Methuen Publishing Limited Reg. No. 3543167

The author has asserted his moral rights.

A CIP catalogue record is available from the British Library.

ISBN 0 413 772128

Typeset by SX Composing DTP, Rayleigh, Essex
Printed and bound in Great Britain by
Cox & Wyman Ltd, Reading, Berkshire

 The publishers are grateful to the Donmar Warehouse
for supplying the cover image.

Frame 312

Keith Reddin

Methuen Drama

Frame 312 premiered at the Donmar Warehouse, London, on 11 March 2002. The cast was as follows:

Lynette (in the 1960s)	Rachel Leskovac
Lynette (in the 1990s)	Margot Leicester
Stephanie	Doraly Rosen
Margie/Marie/Doris	Katherine Parkinson
Tom/Roy/Agent Barry	Matt Bardock
Graham	Nicky Henson

Director Josie Rourke
Designer Tom Piper
Lighting Designer David Plater
Sound Designer Matt McKenzie for Autograph

Characters

Lynette (in the 1960s – early twenties)
Lynette (in the 1990s – early fifties)
Stephanie (early twenties)
Margie/Marie/Doris (mid-twenties)
Tom/Roy/Agent Barry (late twenties)
Graham (mid-fifties)

The play takes place in the early sixties and mid-nineties. Lynette is played by two actresses, one in her early twenties and one in her early fifties.

Act One

Scene One

The 1960s. **Lynette** *at her desk at* Life *magazine.* **Margie** *stands by the desk.*

Margie   It wasn't my birthday or anything. After dinner at the table, he says here, and from his coat pocket he takes out this box and he hands it to me.

Lynette   Just like that?

Margie   With the dirty plates and everything on the table. And I said Henry, let me at least clear the dishes, but he says no first you gotta open my present. (*She shows off new watch.*)

Lynette   It's beautiful.

Margie   Then I start to think.

Lynette   About what?

Margie   It's not as if we can afford these kinds of . . . gestures.

Lynette   It was a present.

Margie   Yes.

Lynette   He didn't . . .

Margie   Maybe he did. Maybe there's another reason.

Lynette   What?

Margie   An ulterior reason.

Lynette   Ulterior.

Margie   Maybe he's feeling guilty.

Lynette   About what, Margie?

Margie   About what I can only speculate.

Lynette   He wanted to do something nice.

Margie   Maybe.

Lynette   I wish somebody would give me a new watch.

Margie   I start thinking about last month.

Lynette   When he was in Chicago?

Margie   Exactly.

Lynette   And you're thinking . . .

Margie   When he wasn't at the Blackstone?

Lynette   Because of the time you called.

Margie   Because of the time I called.

Lynette   OK.

Margie   And later he says he just changed his room. Because it's too close to the elevator, all night he hears the elevator doors open and close, he can't sleep, but when I call, the desk clerk tells me he's not in the room, the original room, and you have to wonder.

Beat.

Lynette   Come on, Margie.

Margie   No, I mean it. You have to. Wonder.

Lynette   It's a really nice watch.

Margie   And I want to believe him. He can be . . . the other day. Watching them unload the coffin on the television.

Lynette   Oh, that was so . . .

Margie   Henry sat with me on the couch, the both of us watching Jackie in her pink dress.

Lynette   With his blood still on it.

Margie   And Jackie holding the children, we're watching it and Henry next to me, and I look over and it looks like he's really sad. He holds my hand tight and I think, I don't ever want you to die, I wouldn't know what to do, but now I don't know.

Lynette   It's a time . . . everybody needs to be strong.

Margie   I know.

Lynette   The country needs us to be strong. We can't give in to . . . dark thoughts.

Margie   He could have called, said I have to change my room.

Lynette   You're right.

Margie   Then he gives me a watch, I have these thoughts. These dark thoughts.

Lynette   He loves you.

Margie   I don't know sometimes.

Lynette   He does. And people. They do these things, it's not always for the reasons we think. Just accept the present and be happy.

Margie   I want to.

Mr Graham *enters.*

Graham   Lynette, I need you to come down to the third floor with me.

Lynette   Of course, Mr Graham.

Margie   Excuse me, I was . . . I had this memo I needed to . . .

Graham   Right.

Margie   I'll talk to you later, Lynette.

Lynette   Sure.

Margie *exits.*

Graham   The ballistics expert is in the conference room. You should . . . you have a pad or something?

Lynette   Right here.

Graham   He says we'll need to review the film a number of times.

Lynette   Did he say how many?

Graham   He didn't say exactly.

Lynette   Oh.

Graham   However many he needs.

Lynette   I understand.

Graham   I . . . I'm not sure what it's going to be like, watching the . . .

Lynette   I'll do whatever you need, Mr Graham.

Graham   Thank you.

Beat.

Lynette   Did you watch the . . . ?

Graham   I saw some of it on the news.

Lynette   I felt so bad.

Graham   We all do. It's a terrible thing what happened. Terrible, but we're a news organisation, we have a responsibility to the public to keep working.

Lynette   I didn't mean . . .

Graham   Of course you didn't.

Lynette   I was only saying . . .

Graham   Yes.

Pause.

Lynette   Will we see him actually . . .

Graham   That's what I understand.

Lynette   I just wanted to know.

Pause.

Graham   I hope you're up to it.

Lynette   I'll do my best.

Graham   Have to keep going.

Lynette   Yes.

Graham   I depend on you, Lynette, you know that, don't you?

Lynette   I do.

Pause.

Graham   Well. Let's get this over with, shall we?

Lights fade.

Scene Two

The 1990s. **Lynette**'s *backyard. Lawn chairs, a table.* **Lynette** *sitting in a chair, looking out. From the back of the house,* **Stephanie** *enters.*

Stephanie   You want some iced tea? Just made some in the kitchen.

Lynette   I'm fine right now, thank you.

Beat.

Stephanie   Should be here soon.

Lynette   He said around four.

Stephanie   Almost four.

Beat.

Lynette   Nice day.

Stephanie   Yes.

Lynette   Turned out quite nice.

Stephanie   Made some sandwiches and some salad. I wasn't sure what . . .

Lynette   Thank you.

Stephanie   Tom and his group, I'm never sure what's allowed.

Lynette   You didn't have to make all that.

Stephanie   It's your birthday.

Lynette   Just another day.

Stephanie *sits down a moment, then stands.*

Lynette   Please just take it easy. Birthdays don't mean anything to me. Really.

Stephanie   All right.

Lynette   It's nice but you shouldn't feel obligated to make a fuss.

Stephanie   It's . . .

Lynette   My birthday, I know.

Stephanie   It's the first . . . without Dad.

Lynette   Yes.

Stephanie   That's all.

Pause.

Lynette   Yes, you're right.

Stephanie   We just thought it might be nice. To spend the day.

Lynette   You're welcome any time.

Stephanie   It's nice of you to say that.

Beat.

Lynette   You know, when I was at the magazine, at *Life*, I always thought of Saturdays as the day we put an issue to

bed. And there was always all this chaos, no matter what, all
this sort of controlled chaos and it was up me to check on
the writers and make sure they got their copy in, and I
would . . . I had to make sure they had enough booze to
finish. Because the truth was most of those writers couldn't
meet their deadlines sober. They had to work almost
eighteen hours straight in a drunken stupor to finish. And I
would go from desk to desk and see how they were doing,
and if they needed another bottle I would go down the street
to this bar we all went to and I'd . . . the owner knew me, he
knew all of us from *Life* magazine, and this man, his name
was Hasek, he was Czech, big man, big chest and
moustache, he'd see me come through his door on a
Saturday afternoon and he'd go into the back and then he'd
come out with several bottles of booze, mainly Scotch. And
I'd walk down the street in the bright Saturday sunshine
with my handbag bulging. I'd go back up to the editorial
offices and hand the bottles out, one by one, so we could
finish another issue of *Life* magazine. And that's what I think
of sometimes when I sit out here on a Saturday.

Pause.

Stephanie   You should have stayed.

Lynette   Where?

Stephanie   At *Life*. You'd probably be running it by now.

Lynette   Who knows.

Stephanie   Tom . . .

Lynette   Yes?

Stephanie   I shouldn't say anything.

Lynette   What is it?

Stephanie   I think Tom's still smoking.

Lynette   He is?

Stephanie   The point is if he starts lighting up while he's here . . . I know I'm supposed to be tolerant but I'm sorry, the studies on second-hand smoke are very impressive.

Lynette   It's just one afternoon.

Stephanie   It's just my life, Mom.

Lynette   Stephanie, don't worry about it. You worry about things.

Stephanie   Excuse me, but there's a lot to worry about.

Lynette   It's his lungs.

Stephanie   Yeah, right, OK, fine.

Lynette   Stephanie, are you . . .

Stephanie   What?

Lynette   Are you all right?

Stephanie   What are you talking about?

Lynette   Well, you're moving around like you're on drugs and I'm hoping if you are on drugs they're drugs that have been prescribed to you by a medical doctor.

Stephanie   I'm not moving around like I'm on drugs.

Lynette   You haven't stopped twitching since you got here. You were in the kitchen slamming cabinets and banging pots, making all that . . . salad. You've never made so much salad. Ever. And it makes me nervous.

Stephanie   I'm making you nervous?

Lynette   Well, yes. That's why I came out here. You're driving me sort of . . . buggy.

Stephanie   OK, I'll stop moving around.

She sits. Tries to stay still. It's hard.

How's this?

Beat.

Mom?

Lynette You're still moving around inside.

Stephanie I can't help it.

She jumps up, faces **Lynette**.

OK, actually I am.

Lynette You are what?

Stephanie On medication.

Lynette You're on medication?

Stephanie For depression.

Lynette You're on depression medication. For how long?

Stephanie Two years.

Lynette Oh.

Stephanie I'm trying to cut back but these family things they make me really depressed and I don't want to totally spin out of control in front of other people, other people meaning you and Tom and his Stepford wife and two little Jon Benet Ramseys, I can't handle them. I try but it just makes me think dark thoughts about knifing them in the face.

Lynette Stephanie, a doctor did give you these drugs?

Stephanie Yes, Mother. It was an actual medical doctor. I did not buy them off some homey in the playground. Although I could. The neighbourhood I'm in, believe me, I could score just about anything. The fact is, like your Czech bar owner, all the drug lords know me. We see each other every day. I could probably work for them if I ever needed some quick cash. I could be a runner, or a lookout for the man. I could be working my way up the drug-dealing food chain, make junior dealer in a few short months.

Lynette Stephanie, don't scare me.

Stephanie I'm not trying to scare you. I'm telling you about my life. Upside, downside living *mi vida loca*. Luckily I have an outlet for all this pent-up angst on a Saturday afternoon. I can go into the kitchen of our tasteful suburban ranch house and make salad. Lots and lots of salad.

Lynette Are you talking to anybody about this?

Stephanie About the salad?

Lynette About your problem.

Stephanie Where do you think the drugs come from? This is America, Mom. Don't ask, don't tell. Medicate.

Lynette And what happens if you . . . stop these drugs.

Stephanie I'm not sure but I imagine it's not pretty.

Lynette Stephanie, you cannot be that . . . depressed about things. You have a good job.

Stephanie You think social work is a good job?

Lynette You're helping people, aren't you?

Stephanie That's the idea.

Lynette You're making a contribution . . . to society.

Stephanie Right. Endless paperwork and visits to abusive foster-parents.

Lynette Then why are you still doing it?

Stephanie It's a living.

Lynette It's more than that.

Stephanie If you say so. I'm sorry, Mom, but I'm not sure I can face everybody today.

Lynette Well, try, Stephanie. Try real hard.

Lights fade.

Scene Three

The 1960s. Conference room at Life *magazine.* **Lynette**, **Graham** *and* **Roy** *sit and view a film. Projector is projecting out front.*

Roy   The motorcade turns on to Elm, at this point moving towards the point of filming. The President and his wife waving to the opposite sides of the street. The car disappears for a second behind a freeway sign and when it emerges, the President is reacting to a shot. His hands go up to his throat. Governor Connally turns to his right, trying to look behind him. His mouth opens. The First Lady places her hand on the President's arm as he begins to sag towards her. The President is bent slightly forward. The right side of his skull explodes. The President is slammed backwards and to the left, where he bounces off the back seat and slides towards the floor. The First Lady climbs towards the rear of the limousine, as a Secret Service agent jumps on to the rear of the car. The car begins to accelerate.

Projector stops. Lights come up on room. Pause.

Breaking it down to individual frames. The President is shot initially at frame 225, Connally struck between frame 231 and frame 234. The President is hit a second time at frame 312.

Pause.

The man who filmed this sequence, Mr Zapruder?

Graham   Lynette . . .

Lynette (*looking at notes*)   He was located on a four-foot-high concrete block at the end of two steps leading to a rise overlooking the motorcade. He stated he lost his balance while testing the camera and asked his secretary to 'steady him and provide support'.

Roy   And you obtained this film yesterday.

Graham   That's right.

Roy   You bought it from Mr Zapruder?

Graham   The magazine paid him one hundred and fifty thousand dollars. Mr Zapruder said he was planning to give the money to the Dallas Police Benevolence Society.

Roy   I see.

Graham   With a suggestion the money goes to Mrs Tippit.

Lynette   Can I say something, Mr Graham?

Graham   What is it?

Lynette   You shouldn't publish it.

Graham   We shouldn't?

Lynette   No . . . It's too upsetting for people.

Graham   But it's history

Lynette   I know.

Graham   We have an obligation.

Lynette   I understand that.

Graham   But we shouldn't publish the stills?

Lynette   Just watching the film, it made me feel sick.

Graham   Would you mind stepping outside for a second, Mr Roy?

Roy   Of course.

Roy *exits.*

Graham   You going to be OK, Lynette?

Lynette   I feel really sick.

Graham   Maybe I . . . I shouldn't have asked you down here.

Lynette   When his head . . . Mr Kennedy's head just, all apart like that. You could see it, and Mrs Kennedy right next to him.

Graham   It's terrible, I know.

Lynette   All apart . . .

Graham   Yes.

Lynette   Don't print this, Mr Graham.

Graham   It's been decided. A few stills from the film. The motorcade, the . . .

Lynette   People need to . . . they don't want to look at this, at him being shot.

Graham   Lynette, why don't you take the rest of the day off?

Lynette   I'm sorry.

Graham   Leave your notes in my office and go home.

Lynette   It's just I feel sick.

Graham   It's hard to take, I know.

Lynette   I'm really sorry.

Graham   That's all right. It's . . . you have to understand, sometimes facts can be unpleasant. Someone being killed, it's very unpleasant. But we have to report it. People want to know.

Lynette   But it's the President. It's President Kennedy. And printing those pictures, you make it like staring at some dead animal. Some animal on the side of the . . .

Graham   It's what we do.

Lynette   Mr Graham, has anybody else seen this?

Graham   The police invited this newsman from CBS who was in Dallas at the time. Dan Rather.

Lynette　What did he say about it?

Graham　Well, he went on the radio yesterday and described what he saw. He told people on the second shot, the President's head went forward with considerable violence.

Lynette　But it went back.

Graham　It did. So you see, Lynette, we need to show these pictures. So people can make up their own minds.

Lynette　I need to get some air.

Graham　You take the rest of the day off.

Lynette　Thank you.

Graham　You just give me your notes. You can type them up tomorrow.

Lynette　I will.

Graham　You understand you can't ever tell anybody what you saw here today.

Lynette　I understand.

Graham　I'm counting on you. You give me your solemn word?

Lynette　I do.

Graham　Well, then, you take the day off.

Lynette　I just want to go home.

Graham　You do that.

Lynette *exits. After a moment* **Roy** *enters.*

Roy　I can understand, it's pretty rough.

Graham　Could you break it down for me, the timing?

Roy　A minimum of 42 frames between each shot. Given the film running at 18.3 frames per second, that's a minimum of 2.3 seconds between shots.

Graham Which means?

Roy That's fast.

Graham How fast?

Roy You ask me, impossibly fast. I don't know many who could fire off three shots in that time.

Graham You're sure?

Roy Well, that's my job. To know these things. You ask me, there was somebody else. Somebody firing from in front. Not far from where the filming took place.

Graham A second gunman.

Roy That's my opinion.

Graham Let's run it one more time.

Lights fade.

Scene Four

The 1990s. **Lynette** *and* **Stephanie** *in the backyard.*

Lynette Just try and behave yourself.

Stephanie I will.

Lynette He's your brother.

Tom *enters from the house.*

Tom Marie's just putting in a video for the kids. They get a little cranky what with the drive.

Stephanie So why not numb them with television.

Tom Hello, Steph.

Lynette How was the drive?

Tom   Not bad. Made it in . . . (*Looks at watch.*) fifty-five minutes. That's from when we hit seventy-eight, not from the actual time we got in the car . . .

Stephanie   Fuck me.

Tom   What?

Lynette   Glad you could all be here.

Tom   Wanted to bring the girls. They love to see their grandma.

Stephanie   Why don't you get a hairpiece?

Tom   What?

Stephanie   I was just wondering if you considered getting a rug.

Lynette   Stephanie . . .

Stephanie   He looks very bald.

Tom   Would you chill?

Lynette   Stephanie, how about you get some iced tea?

Stephanie   But we're making conversation.

Lynette   Then why don't you see if Marie needs any help?

Stephanie   With what?

Lynette   With the children.

Stephanie   You trust me?

Lynette   Stephanie, please.

Stephanie *exits.*

Tom   Not my fault I'm . . . didn't Grandad lose most of his hair by the time he was forty?

Lynette   Before that, I think.

Tom   So it's hereditary.

Lynette   Yes.

Pause.

Tom   So. Having a good birthday?

Lynette   Yes.

Tom   Good weather.

Lynette   Pretty good so far.

Tom   That's good.

Lynette   You just got back from somewhere, didn't you?

Tom   Seminar for all the senior adjusters.

Lynette   Where was it again?

Tom   Dallas.

Lynette   Right.

Tom   Stayed at the new Sheraton. Really great room.

Lynette   How nice.

Tom   Right downtown. Not far from that old book depository.

Lynette   The what?

Tom   The book depository. Where, you know, what's-his-name shot Kennedy.

Lynette   Did you go?

Tom   Where?

Lynette   To the book depository.

Tom   I did, it's a . . . kind of museum. Walk up to the window on the sixth floor, look out. Got a gift shop. Sell all these books, videos. Every kind of wacko theory. Still, it was interesting.

Lynette   I've seen pictures.

Tom   It's smaller than I imagined.

Lynette   What did you imagine?

Tom   I don't know. Something bigger.

Lynette   Did you walk around? Outside by the Plaza.

Tom   Didn't really have time.

Lynette   You had seminars.

Tom   All three days.

Lynette   I've never been to Dallas.

Tom   It's OK.

Lynette   Never really wanted to go.

Tom   It's just a city.

Lynette   I suppose.

Tom   Better to take that cruise up to Alaska.

Lynette   You and Marie should do that.

Tom   Some day.

Lynette   We really enjoyed it. Your father and I.

Tom   Mom, before Marie comes out, there's something I wanted to . . .

Lynette   What?

Tom   We're thinking of getting a new house.

Lynette   You just got the one you're living in, what, two years ago?

Tom   Three actually. Marie feels like we need more space.

Lynette   She does?

Tom   And that means finding a buyer for the house and I don't know how long that might take.

Lynette   It's a beautiful house.

Tom   Sure, but Marie and I feel we need a bigger . . . and we put a bid on this nice place about twenty minutes from here.

Lynette   Uh-huh.

Tom   It's a really great place. Lots of room.

Lynette   Twenty minutes from here?

Tom   Over in Franklin.

Lynette   Sure, that's a very nice area.

Tom   The thing is, till we have a definite buyer on the house, the house we're in now, finances are a little tight.

Lynette   I thought . . .

Tom   Mom, this year we . . . we kind of haven't met . . .

Lynette   What?

Tom   And Marie and I . . . well, I said I'd see how you felt.

Lynette   What are you talking about?

Tom   We could use a little help right now.

Lynette   What kind of help?

Tom   Well, some help.

Lynette   With getting this new house?

Tom   It's a short-term thing. I'm sure we'll find a buyer real soon.

Lynette   What are you asking, Tom?

Tom   A little help, you know.

Lynette   You need me to co-sign?

Tom   Not exactly.

Lynette   Then what?

Tom   See, things haven't been what we expected this year
. . . and what with the girls starting school, that private
school is not cheap, let me tell you, but we looked into a lot
of schools; this is the best around, you can't stint on
education . . .

Lynette   Tom, what do you need?

Tom   A loan.

Pause.

Lynette   I see.

Tom   Just for a little bit.

Lynette   What kind of loan?

Tom   Seventy-five thousand.

Lynette   What?

Tom   That's what I figured we'd need to . . . we're
stretched a little thin right now and . . .

Lynette   Tom, I don't have that kind of money.

Tom   But you do, Mom. I was the one took care of all the
taxes and stuff after Dad . . . and I know what's liquid right
now . . .

Lynette   But seventy-five thousand?

Tom   I know that sounds like a lot.

Lynette   It is a lot.

Tom   Not when you're making an investment like a new
home.

Lynette   Maybe you shouldn't have done this.

Tom   Well, it's a little late for that, Mom. Look, it's only
short-term.

Lynette   I don't know.

Tom   What do you mean?

Lynette   I mean that is a lot of money.

Tom   Not really.

Lynette   Tom, tell me the truth, how are things right now? With you?

Pause.

Tom   We're in a little, I kept thinking things are going to turn around . . .

Lynette   They will.

Tom   But right now . . .

Lynette   Are you in trouble, Tom?

Tom   No.

Lynette   Are you?

Tom   I don't like coming to you like this.

Marie *and* **Stephanie** *enter.*

Marie   Happy birthday, Lynette.

She goes to hug **Lynette**. **Tom** *lights up a cigarette.*

Stephanie   I thought you said you quit.

Tom   I never said that.

Stephanie   You did, Tom. Last time you were here you said you were quitting.

Tom   Well, I'm not right now.

Stephanie   We can see.

Tom   Hey, Steph, cut me some slack, OK?

Stephanie   Cut you some slack?

Tom   Just once.

Marie   Get you anything, Lynette?

Stephanie   How about an ashtray for your husband.

Tom   Fine, you made your point.

He throws his cigarette down, grinds it out with his foot.

Stephanie   Thank you.

Marie   You and Tom catching up?

Lynette   Yes, we were.

Stephanie   You tell Tom I'm on medication?

Marie   You seem wound up.

Tom   Wound up is not the word.

Lynette   Everybody sit down, please.

They all pull up chairs and sit. Beat.

Marie   Somebody has a birthday card!

*She hands **Lynette** a card.*

Lynette   Thank you.

Marie   The girls made it themselves. For their grandma.

Lynette   Really.

Marie   Go ahead, read it.

*They all look at **Lynette**.*

Lynette (*reading the card*)   'For our grandmother. With lots of kisses, with lots of love, here's birthday wishes, for blue skies above. Happy birthday from Annie and Roberta.'

Stephanie   Your kids wrote that?

Marie   They did.

Stephanie   It doesn't really scan.

Lynette   Stephanie . . . Thank you, Marie. I didn't know the girls could write yet.

Tom   They didn't actually write it, they don't know how to write . . .

Marie   They sort of dictated it to me.

Lynette   I see, well, it's a lovely card.

Marie   Yes.

Long pause.

Lynette   Tom said you had a nice drive.

Marie   Yes. Made it in about fifty-five minutes. That's from when we hit seventy-eight, not the actual time we got in the car.

Pause.

Stephanie   I'm on medication because I suffer from depression. If anybody is interested.

Tom   We're not.

Stephanie   I'm suffering from depression because I feel my life is a big pile of shit.

Marie   Stephanie, you don't really think that.

Stephanie   But I do. Every day in my work I see fucked-up kids and their alcoholic parents, and day after day it's nothing but standing in people's living rooms with televisions blasting and people yelling and smashing things and all this suffering, and I feel there is no God, and when I tell people this, people meaning professional people, they prescribe various medications to shut me the fuck up. How are the kids, Marie?

Marie   Fine, they started school.

Lynette   Everybody should . . .

Tom   What, Mom?

Lynette   Everybody . . . I have something I have to show you.

Tom   What is it?

Lynette   Because I have wanted to tell somebody for a very long time.

Stephanie   Tell us what?

Lynette   I'll be right back.

Lights fade.

Scene Five

The 1960s. **Lynette** *and* **Graham** *in* **Mr Graham**'s *office.*

Graham   You need some money for a cab to the station?

Lynette   I can walk.

Graham   I want you to take a cab. I'll feel better.

Lynette   It's only a short walk.

Graham   I understand. Look, here's a ten . . .

Lynette   Mr Graham, I have money.

Graham   You feel better write out a receipt or something, make it official.

Pause.

My wife, she was watching television with my son when Oswald was . . .

Lynette   God.

Graham   Coming through the police station. It was on television. And the thing is, death, it's confusing at that age. He's five.

Lynette   My mother died when I was five.

Graham   I'm sorry.

Lynette   It was just my father and me then.

Graham   My father and I.

Lynette What?

Graham I believe it's my father and I.

Lynette I think you say, I'd say me, if it was just me, I wouldn't say I about myself, so if it was my father and I, I mean, me . . .

Graham You might be right.

Lynette Anyway, we were on our own.

Graham Must have been hard.

Lynette It was.

Graham I bet.

Lynette Not like Mrs Kennedy.

Graham No.

Lynette The whole world watching. And the children.

Graham So it was all right? You and your father?

Lynette I was his little housekeeper.

Graham Ah.

Lynette From the time I was six or seven.

Graham That's something.

Lynette Started doing the cooking.

Graham What did you cook?

Lynette Simple stuff. I wasn't very good.

Graham You were a child. I make quite a chilli.

Lynette You do?

Graham Learned it when I was in the army. Stationed in Texas. San Antonio.

Lynette The Alamo.

Graham Right you are.

Lynette   You know that Patsy Cline song, 'San Antonio Rose'?

Graham   No.

Lynette   It's a really good song.

Graham   I'm not much on popular music.

Lynette   Well, she's great.

Graham   Is she?

Lynette   She's country western, actually.

Graham   None of that rock and roll for you, eh?

Lynette   I like all kinds of music.

Graham   If one plays good music, people don't listen. And if one plays bad music, people don't talk. Oscar Wilde.

Lynette   Uh-huh.

Graham   I don't know what he'd make of Patsy Cline.

Lynette   Well, she's really great. You should get a record of hers some time.

Graham   Maybe I will.

Pause.

It means a lot, you doing this. It's a very important duty.

Lynette   As an American.

Graham   Yes.

Lynette   I'm still nervous.

Graham   Of course you are. Anybody would be.

Lynette   To be carrying it. In my purse like this.

Graham   But that's why it's safe. Nobody will suspect a young lady like you.

Lynette   I guess not.

Graham   Just a few hours and it will be over.

Lynette   And they'll be at Union Station?

Graham   Right there to meet you at the gate.

Lynette   And then they take me over to the FBI building.

Graham   Here's the names of the agents meeting you. You be sure they produce proper identification.

Lynette   Like a badge.

Graham   Like a badge.

Lynette   So it's official.

Graham   They'll take you over. To Mr Hoover. You give him the film personally.

Lynette   All right.

Graham   You know what Mr Hoover looks like?

Lynette   I've seen pictures, sure.

Graham   I met him once.

Lynette   Did you?

Graham   Several years ago.

Pause.

Well, you hand that film to him.

Lynette   Right.

Graham   He's . . . shorter in real life.

Lynette   Is he?

Graham   And heavier.

Lynette   I wouldn't know.

Graham   I found him very unpleasant, actually. But you'll meet him yourself.

Lynette   Pretty soon.

Graham   He smelled of alcohol. Of course, it was at a cocktail party so maybe that was the reason.

Lynette   Maybe.

Graham   Some day, when this all gets sorted out, the investigation, you'll be able to tell people, your friends and family, you met Mr Hoover. You brought something very important all the way to Washington and handed it to him personally.

Lynette   But until then?

Graham   For national security. You'll need to keep all of this to yourself.

Lynette   You think he did it? Oswald. You think he's the one shot the President?

Graham   That's what the authorities say.

Lynette   But what do you think?

Graham   Me?

Lynette   Do you believe he's the one?

Graham   I don't know, Lynette.

Lynette   I don't think he did it.

Graham   Why do you say that?

Lynette   Him being shot that way. At the police station. He kept saying he was the patsy, he was set up. How'd they get to him, with all those policemen? How'd they get in there to kill him?

Graham   Who's 'they'?

Lynette   Them, the people who did it.

Graham   You think there's more than one person involved? Well, who do you think they are?

Lynette   I don't know.

Graham   Anything's possible, Lynette.

Lynette   They could have gotten someone to . . . because it wasn't only Oswald. You saw, Kennedy, he was shot from two different places. From the front and back. From two different locations.

Graham   We'll let the FBI look at the film.

Lynette   But will they tell us the truth?

Pause.

What's going to happen to me?

Graham   Nothing is going to happen.

Lynette   We're the only other people to see that movie.

Graham   Yes, we are.

Lynette   We're the only people. We . . . we know things. What if they try . . . like with Oswald? So we can't tell what we saw.

Graham   That's not going to happen.

Lynette   They can get at people anywhere. On the street, in a bar, a police station. Nowhere is safe.

Graham   Lynette . . .

Lynette   Things are so confusing.

Graham   I know.

Lynette   Maybe they don't want people to know too much. .

Graham   You don't have to be afraid of that.

Lynette   When I hand over the film to them, then they'll know who I am.

Graham   They don't know you actually saw the film.

Lynette   But what if they make me tell them? Tell them what I know?

Graham   Lynette, calm down, that's not going to happen.

Lynette   But what if I don't come back?

Graham   You will. You'll be back tonight. You just hand over the film and come right back. Listen, you call me as soon as you hand it to them. You call me and tell me you're on your way home. I'll wait here for your call. I'll . . . I'll phone my wife and say I've got to stay here a little late and you just phone me . . . Lynette, it's going to be fine.

Lynette   I don't want to die.

Graham   You're not going to.

Lynette   We're the only ones . . .

Graham   You better head over to the station.

Lynette   All right.

Graham   You'll be back tonight.

Lynette   I'll call.

Graham   Everything's going to be fine.

Pause.

Lynette   The thing is . . .

Graham   What?

Lynette   What if I disappeared? Without a trace.

Graham   What are you talking about?

Lynette   I mean, nobody would really notice I was gone. I don't have any family to speak of. And there's people here at the office, and you, but if I was here one day and gone the next, who would really miss me? No one.

Graham   You have to stop talking like this.

Lynette   My life, I'd fall through the cracks. And that's why I'm scared of what might happen.

Graham   I'd look for you.

Lynette   Would you, Mr Graham?

Graham   I would.

Lynette   Thanks for saying that.

Graham   It's true.

Lynette   Thank you.

Graham   Maybe I should have asked someone else.

Lynette   Who else is there?

Graham   I could have asked somebody else.

Lynette   But would they disappear as easily as me?

Graham   Lynette, I don't know why you talk like this.

Lynette   I'll call you when I get there.

Graham   You do that.

Lynette   Thank you for trusting me.

Graham   I do.

Lynette   I try not to trust anyone.

Lights fade.

Scene Six

The 1960s. Train station in Washington DC. **lynette** *and* **Agent Barry**.

Barry   Miss Porter?

Lynette   Excuse me?

Barry   You are Lynette Porter, right?

Lynette   Yes, I am.

Barry   I'm Agent Barry. From the Federal Bureau of Investigation.

Lynette   Could I see some identification, please?

Barry   Identification?

Lynette   Your . . . badge.

Barry   Of course.

He flashes an ID.

Lynette   I'm sorry, could I see that again, please? You did that very quickly and I'd like to make sure you're who you say you are.

Barry   I'm from the Federal Bureau of Investigation, ma'am.

Lynette   I'd just like to make sure.

Beat.

Could you let me see that again?

Beat.

I'm not going to run away with it, for God's sake.

Barry *hands her his ID.*

Barry   You can see . . .

Beat.

Miss Porter?

Lynette   I just wanted to make sure.

Barry   Did you have a nice train ride?

Lynette   As a matter of fact I did not, not really.

Barry   I'm sorry.

Lynette   I kept thinking you people had someone on the train.

Barry   My people?

Lynette   The FBI.

Barry   We didn't have anyone on that train.

Lynette   No?

Barry   No, just me. Waiting at the station.

Lynette   You're sure?

Barry   As far as I know, it's just me.

Lynette   There was this man. On the train. He was sitting across from me. He kept asking for the time.

Barry   Maybe he just wanted to know the time.

Lynette   He was wearing a watch. You see, I notice these things.

Barry   I'm sure you do.

Lynette   He was wearing a watch and he asks me for the time. Every so often.

Barry   Maybe his watch stopped.

Lynette   I don't think so.

Barry   It's certainly possible. Now, if you would just follow me . . .

Lynette   Where are we going?

Barry   Just outside the station, Miss Porter. We have a car.

Lynette   Who is this we?

Barry   Another agent.

Lynette   From the FBI?

Barry   That's correct.

Lynette   And what is his name?

Barry   The man driving the car?

Lynette   Yes, what is his name? Because, you see, I have the names of the people to meet me at the station. I have

written these names down and I'm not going anywhere until
you tell me this other person's name.

Barry   Flag.

Lynette   Agent Flag?

Barry   Yes.

Lynette   Is that his real name?

Barry   Yes, it is.

Lynette   His actual name?

Barry   Yes, it's Charles Flag.

Lynette   His name is Flag and he's an agent with the FBI.

Barry   Believe me, he gets kidded about it all the time.

Lynette   I suppose he does.

Barry   Guess he felt with a name like that he should be
doing some sort of service for his country.

Lynette   If you say so.

Barry   So why don't we just head out to the car, Miss
Porter.

Beat.

Why don't we just take a short drive over to the Bureau.

Lynette   Do you know why I'm here?

Barry   I just know I'm to escort you over to the Bureau.

Lynette   I'm meeting your boss, Mr Hoover.

Barry   Well, we shouldn't keep him waiting, he's a very
busy man.

Lynette   He'll wait for me.

Barry   I really think . . . could I have my, my
identification card, please?

He holds out his hand; **Lynette** *gives him back his ID.*

Barry   Thank you.

Lynette   I suppose they gave a description of me. To know who to meet at the station.

Barry   That's right.

Lynette   And do I match it? The description you got?

Barry   Yes.

Lynette   How did they describe me?

Barry   How you look, Miss Porter. It was a very accurate physical description.

Lynette   Really?

Barry   Yes. Now why don't we move outside.

Lynette   Will you be escorting me back here afterwards?

Barry   My job is just to meet you here and take you over to the Bureau.

Lynette   I see.

Barry   I'm sure you just want to get home as soon as possible.

Lynette   Maybe I'll be staying on a bit. I might want to stay and see the sights. The Lincoln Memorial. The Smithsonian Museum. Arlington Cemetery.

Barry   Miss Porter, please.

Lynette   I know it's not cherry blossom time but still I hear Washington can be very pretty.

Barry   It's a very interesting city.

Lynette   He'll wait for me, Agent Barry. Mr Hoover will wait till I'm ready to see him. Because I have something he wants.

Barry   Miss Porter, I don't want to argue with you, I want you to follow me outside . . .

Barry *steps towards* **Lynette**.

Lynette   Don't you dare touch me.

Barry   I wasn't.

Lynette   Don't you try to manhandle me into the back seat of some dark sedan, speed off through some back streets, think about leaving my body in some alley.

Barry   I'm just trying to do my job. Please let me do my job, Miss Porter.

Lynette   And your name is?

Barry   Agent Barry.

Lynette   Your first name. Tell me your first name and we can go. Remember, I saw your identification card.

Barry   Chet.

Lynette   It's Chester.

Barry   Yes.

Lynette   Chester Barry. You see, I wanted to make sure. I have a job to do also, Chester.

Beat.

You look like a Chet, not a Chester.

Barry   Well, we settled that.

Lynette   Yes, we did.

Barry   This way.

Lynette   How long you been with the Bureau, Chet?

Barry   Quite a while . . .

Lynette   Have a nice pension plan?

Barry   This way, Miss Porter.

Lynette   You go first.

Barry   Let's go together, shall we?

Lynette   All right.

Barry   You're really making this more difficult than you need to.

Lynette   It's the only time in my life when I'm able to.

Lights fade.

Scene Seven

The 1990s. **Lynette** *stands on the back steps. She holds a small package.* **Tom**, **Stephanie** *and* **Marie** *look at her.*

Lynette   It was late in the afternoon. I remember thinking, just another hour or so and we can go home. There were some things to pick up from the cleaners on the way. I had some chops I wanted to thaw for dinner. At first I thought it was some sort of joke, a joke in bad taste, but then I looked around and I could see by the expression on people's faces it wasn't a joke. It had just come over the wire service, people were talking so fast, trying to understand exactly what had happened. It was all very confusing.

And over the years, when you met someone, at a bar or waiting for a train, and you got to talking, trying to make polite conversation, often the topic would come up. Where were you when you first heard the news he had been shot? And I'd say, at my desk on the fourth floor of the Time Life building in New York City.

And later, after I'd had my meal of lamb chops and mint jelly, on the television they showed them loading the coffin into the plane. It was night at the airfield and there she was, Mrs Kennedy, in her dress with his blood still on it. And then they flew back to Washington and we went to bed and got up for work the next morning.

Pause.

Tom   They always show old clips on the television. On the anniversary of the assassination.

Lynette   It's over thirty years.

Tom   I was telling Mom I was in Dallas and I went to the book depository.

Stephanie   Right.

Tom   You can go up to the window.

Lynette   On the sixth floor.

Tom   Right. Where Oswald shot him.

Stephanie   What makes you think Oswald shot him?

Tom   Who do you think did it, then?

Stephanie   Take your pick.

Tom   They proved it was him.

Stephanie   Nothing's proved.

Tom   It was him. It's just hard for people to accept one crazy fuck with a gun killing the President.

Marie   You said you had something to show us, Lynette.

Lynette   Oh, yes.

Tom   Everything all right, Mom?

Lynette   Everything's fine.

Tom   You look a little pale.

Stephanie   She said she was fine.

Tom   Sit down, Mom.

Lynette   Yes.

Marie   What is it? What do you want to show us?

Lynette *moves from the steps into the yard. The others watch her.*

Lynette   I . . . I wanted to share something with you.

Marie   What is it?

Lynette *moves to one of the lawn chairs, sits.*

Lynette   Let me just have some iced tea.

She drinks some iced tea.

Tom   It's funny talking about . . . I was just in Dallas. Standing on the grassy knoll.

Marie   You didn't bring anything back.

Tom   What should I bring back? Some sod from the grassy knoll?

Marie   Something for the girls.

Tom   I was there for business, Marie.

Lynette   You know, I was one of the first people to see it.

Stephanie   See what, Mom?

Lynette   The film.

Stephanie   What film?

Lynette   Of Kennedy being shot.

Tom   You mean that Oliver Stone movie? I tried to watch it, it was so fucking long.

Lynette   No, the actual film.

Tom   Which actual film?

Lynette   Of Kennedy being shot.

Marie   What is she talking about?

Stephanie   The Zapruder film?

Lynette   Yes.

Tom   You saw the Zapruder film? When was this?

Lynette   It was part of my job.

Tom   What, you were on the Warren Commission?
(*Laughs.*)

Lynette   I watched the film. Over and over. Two days
after he was shot. Before anybody else saw it.

Beat.

Just my boss and myself and a ballistics expert we had hired.

Stephanie   We didn't know.

Lynette   How could you? I wasn't allowed to say
anything.

Tom   You're joking, right?

Lynette   All this time I never told anyone. Not anyone.
Not even your father.

Beat.

And it was an accident. He didn't know he would be filming
history. He was just there to watch the motorcade, he was
trying out his new camera.

She moves to the back steps.

He was standing on a four-foot-high concrete block at the
end of the steps leading up to the rise. His secretary had to
steady him. Only twenty seconds. That's how long the film
is.

Tom   That's all?

Lynette   Running at 18.3 frames per second, that's only
2.3 seconds between each shot. Would you like to see it?

Stephanie   See it?

Marie   What, a video?

Lynette   Not a video. No, we can watch it here.

Tom   Here?

Lynette   I can show it to you.

Marie   How can you do that?

Tom   Mom?

Lynette   Because I have it.

Pause.

Tom   You have the . . .

Lynette   I have the film. The actual film.

She holds out the package.

Stephanie   You have the . . .

Lynette   The film. This is it. Right here.

Lights fade.

Act Two

Scene One

The 1990s. **Lynette**, **Stephanie**, **Tom** *and* **Marie** *in the backyard.*

Lynette   Sometimes, late at night I would watch it. I would wait till everyone was asleep, and I'd go into the basement and I would watch the film.

Tom   A copy. You watched a copy.

Lynette   No, the real film. I've wanted to say something for a long time. And now, with your father gone . . . I'm . . . I'm all alone here. Alone in the house and I've had this time to think. To think about the things I want to tell you. Would you like to watch it?

Tom   Mom, are you angry at me? About what we talked about before?

Marie   Maybe we should see how the girls are . . .

Tom   Is this what this is about?

Lynette   I could set it up for you.

Tom   Because I could understand how you might be upset about what we talked about.

Marie   Tom . . .

Tom   Marie, why don't you . . .

Marie   What?

Tom   So you're saying the government doesn't have the actual film?

Lynette   Yes.

Stephanie   You have the actual film.

Lynette The magazine bought the film from Mr
Zapruder. Right after the shooting. There was a stringer
from *Life* at Dealey Plaza and he heard Zapruder say I think
I got the whole thing on film. And we bought it from him
that afternoon. And two days later we viewed the film in
New York, before we handed it over to the FBI.

Marie But it was a copy.

Lynette They didn't know that.

Tom Mom, you cannot have the actual film.

Lynette But I do, Tom.

Tom It's just not possible.

Lynette Why not?

Stephanie Are you calling Mom a liar?

Lynette He's not doing that.

Marie Wouldn't that be worth a lot of money?

Lynette I imagine it would.

Tom Look, I'm not saying you're . . . but you must be
confused.

Lynette I'm not confused. You see, I've watched the
original, many times, and I've compared it with the film
that's been released and they're not the same. The obvious
reason they changed it is that they did it to prove it was a
lone gunman. That's the most obvious justification.

Marie It must be worth a lot. And you've had it here.

Lynette If people knew, back then, knew I had it, well,
there's no telling what might happen.

Tom What are you talking about?

Marie You would have to be silenced.

Tom Marie, do not encourage her.

Lynette   It's possible.

Tom   That does not happen.

Stephanie   You don't think our government kills people?

Tom   Our government doesn't . . . OK, maybe people in
. . . in hostile countries, but not its own citizens.

Stephanie   Wake up.

Tom   Would you stop that shit?

Marie   Do you think they know?

Tom   Who is this 'they' everybody keeps talking about?

Marie   Them.

Stephanie (*to* **Lynette**)   You asked if we wanted to see
the film.

Tom   I don't.

Stephanie   You're not even curious?

Tom   Look, I understand Dad's dying has been a terrible
. . . and you're probably feeling . . .

Lynette   You think I'm crazy, Tom?

Tom   I didn't say that.

Marie   I don't think she's crazy.

Lynette   Thank you.

Tom   You just come out with this and, I'm sorry, but I
find it a little hard to swallow.

Marie   I think it's wild.

Stephanie   Wild?

Tom   Marie, I thought you were going to check on the
kids.

Marie   Why don't you?

Tom   Because you said you were going to . . .

Marie   They have names, Tom.

Tom   What?

Marie   Your 'kids' have names.

Tom   Of course they do.

Marie   Then what are their names?

Tom   Why are you doing this?

Marie   Say their names, Tom. The names of your kids.

Tom   I know their . . . Annie and . . . and . . .

Marie   Roberta.

Tom   I know.

Marie   Then why don't you call them by their names? Say Annie and Roberta.

Lynette   I could go and . . .

Tom   Stop it.

Marie   Just say their names,Tom.

Tom   Annie And Roberta, Annie and Roberta, now fucking stop!

Pause.

I'll be inside.

He exits into the house. Pause.

Marie   I'm sorry about that.

Lynette   Tom is just confused right now.

Marie   We never knew . . . any of what you were talking about.

Lynette   Of course not.

Marie   It was a secret, right?

Lynette   Yes, and I understand everybody needs some time to take this in.

Stephanie   We do.

Lynette   It's a big thing.

Stephanie   It's just . . . don't take this the wrong way, but it's just hard to think of you as involved in . . . I mean, we think of you, as you know, Mom. Mom who drove me to ballet practice and made pot roast, and it's a bit of a leap to connect you with this conspiracy shit.

Beat.

Actually, it's a big leap.

Marie   Yes.

Lynette   People don't really want to know.

Marie   We do.

Lynette   You don't, though.

Stephanie   What don't we want to know?

Lynette   Anything, really.

Marie   You think that?

Lynette   I didn't ask for any of it. One afternoon my boss asks me to bring my pad and pencil and take notes, and then my life is changed. I became part of a chain of events bigger than anything I imagined my life would include. I've spent almost thirty years trying to forget.

Stephanie   Did you?

Lynette   I want to forget. Forget all the times I saw that motorcade. But it won't go away. It never goes away. I see it, over and over, in my mind. Then I think I remember a detail and I have to check, I watch the movie, things don't match, they don't add up, something's different from before, some tiny movement, a turn of the head, an expression, I watch the movie and it never goes away. Never. It's a snuff

film. It's the most famous snuff film in history. And I
can't . . . I can't save anyone's life.

Pause.

Marie   I just . . .

Lynette   Yes.

Marie   I'll see how Tom's doing.

Lynette   You do that.

Marie   I'll be . . .

She exits.

Stephanie   I'm sorry.

Lynette   What are you sorry about?

Stephanie   That it messed you up.

Lynette   A lot of things can 'mess you up'.

Stephanie   You know what I'm saying.

Lynette   Insight from my drug addict daughter.

Stephanie   The drugs are prescribed.

Lynette   That makes me feel so much better.

Beat.

Do you believe me?

Stephanie   About the film? I suppose I do.

Lynette   Tom doesn't.

Stephanie   Would you if you were him?

Lynette   Probably not.

Stephanie   But then he's in denial about a lot of things.

Lynette   He's not in denial.

Stephanie   Please . . .

Lynette   He wants to get a new house.

Stephanie   He does? Well, that should solve all his problems.

Pause.

Lynette   I'll tell you something, Stephanie. I've . . . I've never felt comfortable with Tom's children. I've tried to.

Stephanie   I know, they're creepy.

Lynette   It's terrible, but I feel like they judge me. They're like little versions of Tom. They watch the way I move, the way I pour iced tea and fix them grilled cheese sandwiches, and it feels like some sort of test. I . . . I feel very relieved when they go home.

Stephanie   Like they're little alien beings observing you.

Lynette   Exactly.

Pause.

Stephanie   Your life here. The life with Dad and us, growing up. What was that?

Lynette   It was the only real thing I had.

Lights fade.

Scene Two

The 1960s. **Lynette** *on the train to New York. Next to her sits* **Doris**.

Doris   They came to the front door.

Lynette   When?

Doris   In the night. You hear the doorbell ring, the first thing you think . . .

Lynette   Something bad has happened.

Doris   They were standing there and I turn on the porch light, and Phil – that's my husband – he's standing next to me . . .

Lynette   Were they in uniform?

Doris   Who?

Lynette   The police.

Doris   No, they were in . . . suits. Dark suits.

Lynette   They were detectives.

Doris   I asked for some sort of identification.

Lynette   To make sure.

Doris   They could be . . .

Lynette   Robbers. Anything. And what did they say?

Conductor *enters.*

Conductor   New York. Next stop is Grand Central Station, New York City.

He exits.

Doris   They said we have some terrible news.

Lynette   Oh.

Doris   And I said, is this about . . . is it about Michael?

Lynette   You knew.

Doris   I thought these people here, in the dead of night . . .

Lynette   Yes.

Doris   Somebody shot him. They shot my brother in some bar. He's in the hospital.

Lynette   But he's alive.

Doris   Nothing makes sense. People shooting each other.

Lynette   Even the President.

Doris   I went to the Capitol. I waited in line to pay my respects.

Lynette   It won't stop here.

Doris   What do you mean?

Lynette   The President, that's only the beginning.

Doris   The beginning of what?

Lynette   Of something terrible.

Beat.

I shouldn't have told you.

Doris   I just want to see my brother.

Lynette   He's alive. Just remember that.

Doris   You're right.

Lynette   Other people might not live.

Doris   What are you saying?

Lynette   Do you know why I went to Washington DC today?

Doris   I don't.

Lynette   I'm going to tell you something. My name is Lynette. Lynette Porter. I want you to remember my name.

Doris   I . . .

Lynette   Say my name.

Doris   Lynette Porter.

Lynette   Remember what I look like.

Doris   I should . . . we're almost at the station.

Lynette   If one day you read in the paper that I died. If they say my car crashed, or I burned in a fire. Remember.

Doris   There are people meeting me.

Lynette   Whatever you read. It's not the truth.

Doris   Why do you say that?

Lynette   Because I know things.

Doris   You're not making sense.

Lynette   They can kill presidents.

Doris   Who?

Lynette   They won't stop there.

Doris   Please . . .

Lynette   What hospital is your brother in?

Doris   I don't understand . . .

Lynette   Tell me the hospital.

Doris   Lennox Hill.

Lynette   And where is it located? The hospital?

Doris   East 75th?

Lynette   Lennox Hill Hospital is located on East 77th street.

Doris   I meant 77th. I was confused . . .

Conductor *enters*.

Conductor   Grand Central, New York. All out for New York City.

Doris   Excuse me?

Conductor   Yes?

Doris   Can you help me?

Conductor   What can I do for you?

Doris   Could you . . . could you get a redcap to help me with my bags? I'm getting off here and I need help.

Conductor   Don't worry.

Doris Thank you.

Sound of train pulling in, bells.

Lynette Just read the paper. If you see my picture, you'll know.

Doris I'm sorry if I . . . I just needed someone to talk to.

Lynette Your brother will recover.

Doris I pray he will.

Lynette Just remember what we talked about. It's important to remember.

Doris I will.

Lynette That's all we can do.

Lights fade.

Scene Three

The 1960s. A table at P.J. Clark's. **Lynette** *and* **Margie**.

Lynette That's not actually her singing, you know.

Margie Sure it is.

Lynette No, I read they have somebody else singing all her songs.

Margie You're telling me that's not Audrey Hepburn singing?

Lynette No.

Margie I could swear it was her.

Lynette A reliable source.

Margie They did a good job.

Lynette They did.

Margie I still enjoyed the movie.

Lynette   Did you see it on Broadway?

Margie   No. Was it different?

Lynette   Not really.

Margie   I would swear she was singing all those songs.

Lynette   You have to admit she's beautiful.

Margie   And sophisticated.

Lynette   Very.

Beat.

Margie   Well, we're making a night of it.

Lynette   We are.

Margie   It's a celebration. Here's to the new editor.

Raises her glass.

Lynette   Assistant to the editor.

Margie   Come on, it's a big deal.

Lynette   It's nice.

Margie   And more money . . .

Lynette   That doesn't hurt.

Margie   And you didn't have to sleep with anybody. You didn't, did you?

Lynette   Cut it out.

Margie   I'm kidding, OK.

Lynette   I work hard.

Margie   I know you do.

Lynette   Let's have another.

Margie   Sounds swell.

Signals for the waiter.

Lynette　I could learn to love Martinis. They make you feel . . .

Margie　Sophisticated.

Lynette　They do.

Margie　And witty.

Lynette　Absolutely.

Margie　Another couple of these and I'll be singing like Audrey Hepburn, except it's somebody else.

Lynette　I could have danced all night.

Margie　Speaking of which, you still seeing what's-his-name?

Lynette　You know his name, Margie.

Margie　Eddie, you still seeing Eddie?

Lynette　Maybe.

Margie　Oh, this is turning into something, huh?

Lynette　We're friends.

Margie　Good friends.

Lynette　We like each other.

Margie　Ding dong the bell is gonna chime.

Lynette　It's not like that.

Margie　Get me to the church on time.

Lynette　Cut that out, why don't you?

Margie　I'm kidding. What, now that you're editor you can't get kidded?

Lynette　Assistant to the assistant . . .

Margie　So excuse me.

Lynette　We like each other.

Margie   I guess you do.

Lynette   He's . . . special.

Margie   He's better than that, he's an engineer.

Lynette   Not just that.

Margie   Where's that waiter?

Lynette   We share the same interests.

Margie   That helps. So is it serious?

Lynette   Maybe.

Margie   I've grown accustomed to his face . . .

Lynette   Maybe we'll . . . I don't know.

Margie   He played football, didn't he?

Lynette   In college.

Margie   You can tell, just looking at him, he's so . . .

Lynette   Yeah.

Margie   I've seen him waiting for you at reception, end of day. Picking you up, going out to dinner.

Lynette   We get along nice.

Margie   Why shouldn't you?

Lynette   No reason I can think of.

Margie   So what's he think about your new job?

Lynette   I haven't told him yet.

Margie   You haven't? He doesn't know you're not a secretary any more?

Lynette   No.

Margie   Why haven't you said anything?

Lynette   I'm . . . I'm waiting for the right time.

Margie   It was me, I'd call him first thing.

Lynette   I'll tell him.

Margie   Boy, I bet he'll be excited.

Lynette   He will.

Margie   So when are you going to break the news?

Lynette   Just waiting for the right time.

Margie   Uh-huh.

Lynette   He's in the middle of this big project, he's kind of focused on that.

Margie   But you're an editor, excuse me, assistant editor.

Lynette   I know.

Margie   At *Life* magazine. News like that, ding dong the bells are gonna chime.

She laughs.

Lynette   Enough, Margie.

Margie   I'm kidding.

Lynette   That's enough, OK. The joke's not funny any more.

Margie   All right.

Lynette   I'll tell him when I tell him.

Margie   I know.

Lynette   There he is, the waiter.

Margie   What?

Lynette   Our waiter.

Margie   Two more.

She indicates another round.

I could swear it was her singing.

Lynette   Well, it's not. Take my word for it.

Margie   I will.

Lynette   I mean, it's the movies, right?

Margie   It is.

Lynette   It's all make-believe anyway.

Lights fade.

Scene Four

The 1990s. **Lynette** *and* **Tom**. *It is late afternoon. The sunlight fading to sunset.*

Tom   I'm sorry.

Lynette   It's all right.

Tom   It's just . . . it's a lot to take in.

Lynette   Yes.

Tom   I mean, there's no reason you would . . . make something like that up.

Lynette   It's not made up, Tom.

Tom   No, of course not.

Lynette   I wanted to protect myself.

Tom   And us.

Lynette   I'm sorry?

Tom   And us. From . . . whatever might happen.

Lynette   I was thinking about myself. About protecting myself. My life.

Pause.

Tom   So what do you do now?

Lynette   What do you mean?

Tom   With the . . . the film. What do you intend to do?

Lynette   I'm not sure.

Tom   Look . . . there's several ways of looking at this.

Beat.

You could come forward, you could take the thing to . . . I don't know, experts. There are all kinds of assassination experts, right?

Lynette   More than you could imagine.

Tom   You could let them see the . . . they could verify it.

Lynette   Maybe.

Tom   Sure, people would disagree on . . . but somebody could, they have processes, scientific processes, to determine age and authenticity. Somebody could make a strong case that you might have the real deal. The actual Zapruder film and all that means.

Lynette   If I handed it over.

Tom   And there would be arguments, sure, and theories about this and that, but somebody would make the case that you had something. Something important.

Lynette   I do, Tom.

Tom   I'm talking about other people. The . . . public. Forgive me but I never got into any of that stuff.

Lynette   I've read a number of books over the years.

Tom   The point is someone would say yes, you have it.

Lynette   They might.

Tom   You could do that, now that you've come forward.

Lynette   I haven't come forward. I've just told you and Marie and Stephanie.

Tom   And nobody else?

Lynette   Just you here.

Tom   The thing is . . . it could be worth a lot of money. To somebody. Some . . . collector.

Lynette   I suppose so.

Tom   You could sell it for a lot of money.

Lynette   I wouldn't do that, Tom.

Tom   You wouldn't?

Lynette   It's not something I could . . . it was given to me. It was entrusted. If I let people know about it, it would be so the truth could be known. For history.

Tom   So you wouldn't consider selling it?

Lynette   No, I couldn't do that.

Tom   But . . . it might be a lot of money.

Lynette   I understand.

Tom   But . . . you wouldn't do something like that. So we could, I guess we could, go to the press or something, tell them you've had it all these years. Or we could . . . we could just pretend we never knew and just go on with our lives.

Tom   Well, we could try. From this point on. Because you tell people now, you'll have every nutbag in the country camping out on the front lawn. People shoving microphones in your face. Banging on the windows.

Lynette   That's possible.

Tom   They'll say all sorts of things. They'd think it was a hoax.

Lynette   Yes.

Tom   Or that you were deluded.

Lynette   Some people might think that.

Tom She's just a deluded, lonely old woman with time on her hands.

Lynette How could they not think that.

Tom Exactly.

Beat.

She just wants attention. So maybe it's best you . . . if you don't want the money, you could stop that from happening by . . .

Beat.

Tom Hey, everybody thinks the original is in Washington, nobody has ever questioned the veracity of . . .

Marie *appears from the back of the house.*

Marie Tom, when are you . . .

Tom In a couple of minutes, Marie.

Marie The girls are getting . . .

Tom I need to finish a few things with my mother, if you don't mind.

Marie But Tom . . .

Tom Marie, just go back inside with Stephanie and let me have a few minutes. Is that too much to ask?

Marie We need to talk, Tom.

Tom We can talk on the ride home.

Beat.

Marie I need to . . .

Tom On the ride home. Thank you.

Marie *looks at him. Exits.*

Tom So what are you thinking?

Lynette I don't know.

Tom   I really think the best thing is to sell the thing.

Lynette   I don't know if I can do that.

Tom   It's really the best thing, you ask me.

Lynette   I never asked you, Tom.

Tom   No.

Lynette   You just told Stephanie and Marie to go inside for a few minutes and then proceeded to lecture me.

Tom   I'm only trying to help.

Lynette   This is something I have to figure out for myself.

Tom   You're . . .

Lynette   For a long time I've . . . the way I did things has been for others.

Tom   That's not true.

Lynette   The fact of the matter is, you don't know everything about my life.

Tom   I lived here.

Lynette   You did.

Tom   I lived here all my . . . till I went away to college.

Lynette   And what did you observe, all those years?

Tom   We were a family. A normal family. Why are you talking like this?

Lynette   You've decided you know so much.

Tom   I don't know why you're acting like this.

Lynette   How am I acting, Tom?

Tom   What, so you've been . . . what, lying to everybody for thirty years? Everything is a lie? Everything you did with me, with, with Dad, that was all a giant lie?

Lynette   Maybe it's time you go, Tom.

Tom   What?

Lynette   It's getting late, and you and Marie and the children have a long drive.

Tom   We . . . you didn't have your cake. We bought you a birthday cake.

Lynette   That's all right.

Tom   I especially got a cake with your name on it, the girls are waiting. It's for you.

Lynette   I'm not in the mood for cake.

Tom   But we planned to make a day of it.

Lynette   I'm tired now.

Tom   It's your birthday . . . I don't understand.

Lynette   That's all right. You should just go home.

Tom   Mom, don't do this.

Lynette   I'd like you to go now. Don't call later, see how I am. I'm fine.

Tom   Wait a minute . . .

Lynette   This is my home now, Tom. You have your own home. Go back to it.

Tom   This is my home. Right here, this is . . .

Marie *appears at the back door.*

Marie   Tom . . .

Tom   I . . . It's time to go, Marie.

Marie   What about the cake?

Tom   Fuck the cake. We're leaving.

He looks at **Lynette***, walks towards the house.*

Lights fade

Scene Five

The 1960s. **Graham***'s office.* **Lynette** *and* **Graham**.

Graham   Thank you for coming in, Lynette.

Lynette   Not at all.

Graham   How do you like the editorial side of things?

Lynette   Really well.

Graham   Everything working out there?

Lynette   Sure.

Graham   I heard a rumour. I heard you're getting married.

Lynette   Well . . .

Graham   Any truth to that rumour?

Lynette   Next month.

Graham   He work here? At the magazine?

Lynette   No.

Graham   So you're getting hitched to a civilian. (*They both smile.*)

Lynette   That's it.

Graham   Where you planning to go on your honeymoon?

Lynette   We talked about Europe but we – Eddie, my fiancé – well, he though we should save up our money. Look towards getting a new house.

Graham   A house?

Lynette   In the suburbs.

Graham   So you'll be commuting.

Lynette   Well, the thing is . . . Eddie and I talked about this, and the thing is, we decided I should . . . he's an

engineer and we . . . with my hours at the magazine we'd
never see much of . . .

Graham   I understand.

Lynette   I'll probably be leaving the magazine soon.

Graham   Well, congratulations. On your impending
nuptials.

Lynette   Thank you.

Graham   It seems I'll be leaving as well.

Lynette   You're retiring?

Graham   Not exactly.

Lynette   Then why . . .

Graham   The fact is I'm sick, Lynette.

Lynette   Oh, I . . .

Graham   The doctors did some tests and I'm . . .

Lynette   Oh, Mr Graham.

Graham   So I wanted to spend what time I . . . with my
wife. It'll be strange, not coming in to the office.

Lynette   I'm so sorry.

Graham   People get sick, Lynette.

Lynette   I don't know what to say.

Graham   There's nothing to say.

Lynette   Do the others . . .

Graham   No, I'm not telling people right now. I just
wanted to let you know.

Lynette   Thank you.

Graham   It's all right. What I've got. It's a very advanced
form. I . . . I don't think I have more than five or six
months.

Lynette   Maybe they made a mistake.

Graham   I don't think so.

Lynette   But you're not that old.

Graham   It's very advanced. There's no reason to these things.

Lynette   Is there anything I can do?

Graham   You can do something for me, Lynette.

Lynette   What is it?

Graham   There's something.

Lynette   Anything you want.

Graham   You remember Mr Roy? Last year, after the assassination.

Lynette   The ballistics expert?

Graham   That's right. Well, I found out he passed away.

Lynette   He did?

Graham   He passed away a few weeks ago.

Lynette   I . . . I didn't know.

Graham   There's no reason you would.

Lynette   How did he die?

Graham   I'm not sure. I believe I read it was some sort of accident. He had an accident driving. And now I . . . and that means you'll be the only one.

Lynette   What do you mean?

Graham   The only one left who saw the original film.

Lynette   The original . . . I don't understand.

Graham   The original Zapruder film.

Lynette   But others have . . . I took the film to the FBI.

Graham   They have a copy.

Lynette   They do?

Graham   I was always afraid of what might happen. With the film. And I was right. The evidence in the commission report, it's not the same as . . . as what we saw that day. The notes from Roy's analysis. They've altered it. Various frames. Length between shots. A few frames to increase time between shots. So it would match up with their findings.

Lynette   Their findings?

Graham   The commission. That it was just Oswald did the shooting.

Lynette   So you . . .

Graham   I gave them a copy. I have the original film.

Lynette   What are you going to do?

Graham   It's what you're going to do, Lynette.

Lynette   What can I . . .

Graham   I'm giving you the film.

Pause.

Lynette   I . . . don't ask me to . . .

Graham   I'm dying, Lynette.

Lynette   Please.

Graham   Hold on to it. Let people see it. Not right away. Not for years. Because no one would believe you now. You know that, don't you, no one would believe you.

Lynette   Yes.

Graham   They'd . . . humiliate you. Slander you. So you have to wait. Till things . . . because right now they want it to go away. Everything that's unsettled or unknown needs to go away. That's the way things are. This is the truth. That's the end of it. The country needs to come together, people need to move on. A Supreme Court judge and his commission says this is the truth.

Lynette   Don't ask this of me.

Graham   Somebody has to hold on to it.

Lynette   I'm getting married next month.

Graham   I understand.

Lynette   I'm leaving the magazine.

Graham   Here it is.

He takes a package from his desk drawer.

Take it, Lynette.

He holds it out to her.

I trust you. More than anyone.

Finally **Lynette** *takes the package.*

Thank you.

Lynette   I'm sorry you're dying.

Graham   We're all dying, Lynette. Every one of us.

Lights fade.

Scene Six

The 1990s. Early evening. **Lynette** *and* **Stephanie**.

Stephanie   Tom's gone.

Lynette   Yes.

Stephanie   Packed up his progeny and hit the road.

Lynette   Did they take the cake?

Stephanie   I'm sorry?

Lynette   The birthday cake? Did they take it with them?

Stephanie   No, it's out in the kitchen.

Lynette   Right.

Stephanie   The girls were disappointed.

Lynette   All that food, just sitting there. I'll wrap it up later.

Stephanie   Mom? What did you say to Tom?

Lynette   When?

Stephanie   Before he left. What did you . . .

Lynette   They're getting a new house. In Franklin.

Stephanie   Really.

Lynette   I said I would help him out.

Stephanie   Help him out how?

Lynette   I would loan him some money. So that he and Marie could get their new house

Stephanie   I see.

Lynette   From the insurance money. That money, I mean, I don't need much. I'm very comfortable, and . . . the money, it's for both of you. That's the way I look at it, that's what money is for. To spend it when you're alive. If I can help you, then . . . all you have to do is ask.

Stephanie   I guess that's the difference between Tom and me.

Lynette   What's that?

Stephanie   I would never ask.

Lynette   No.

Stephanie   So give him the money. I don't care.

Pause.

Lynette   He . . . he and your father. They got on well.

Stephanie   Yes.

Lynette   When your father was in the hospital . . . sharing jokes, talking about, I don't know, sports and stocks and there was a time I thought that . . . but that never seemed to happen with us, did it? We never really . . .

Stephanie   No.

Lynette   Was it me?

Stephanie   It was both of us.

Lynette   I've tried to be good.

Stephanie   That's the problem, Mom. That you have to try.

Lynette   I suppose.

Stephanie   And then I try to be a . . . daughter, whatever.

Lynette   We haven't really got the hang of it yet, have we?

Stephanie   Not yet.

Lynette   I was brought up a certain way.

Beat.

Fit in and . . . people like me, women, it was before things changed. You were supposed to build a family.

Stephanie   Yes.

Lynette   That's all I meant.

Stephanie   Why didn't you stay at the magazine?

Lynette   At *Life*?

Stephanie   Why did you leave?

Lynette   I was getting married.

Stephanie   You once told me you were promoted to some kind of editorial position.

Lynette   A minor editorial position. A glorified assistant.

Stephanie   You could have stayed.

Lynette   I don't know, Stephanie.

Stephanie   You could have done it. People did.

Lynette   I . . . I thought I wanted to fit in. Be normal. Live out here, not work in some office in the city. I thought that was enough back then. You would meet someone. Someone who would take you away from the office. Have a nice house and kids. But what do I have now?

Stephanie   You have the Zapruder film.

Lynette   Well, I have that.

Stephanie   So you were never just like everybody else around here.

Lynette   But I tried to be.

Stephanie   You never did that good a job of it. Why didn't you ever tell us, about the film?

Lynette   Time just . . . passed.

Stephanie   But now . . .

Lynette   Yes.

Stephanie   And you trust us? To keep quiet?

Lynette   You will.

Stephanie   Maybe I'm not like you.

Lynette   You're not that different from me.

Stephanie   Mom, excuse me, but we couldn't be more different.

Lynette   I don't think we are and I don't think you'll say anything.

Stephanie   I'd like to see it, though.

Lynette   See the film?

Stephanie   Yes.

Lynette   You think you've seen it. On the television or . . . but you haven't really. Not the actual thing. The actual thing, right in front of you. You don't forget that.

Stephanie   Will you show it to me?

Lynette   You really want to?

Stephanie   If I could.

Lynette   All right.

Lynette *goes into the house.* **Stephanie** *walks about the yard. After a bit,* **Lynette** *enters with old super 8mm projector.*

Lynette   Remember this?

Stephanie   God, yes.

Lynette   Used to show all those stupid movies of our trips your father took.

Stephanie   Disneyland.

Lynette   Exactly.

Stephanie   I haven't seen that thing in for ever.

Lynette   I've had to be very careful, the film, it's so old . . . well, anyway.

She positions the projector out front.

We'll just look at it against the garage wall. Like a drive-in movie.

Lynette *starts the film. She and* **Stephanie** *look out towards the audience. After thirty seconds, the film ends.* **Lynette** *turns off the projector. Silence.*

Lynette   There it is.

Stephanie   He . . . you see it, right there, his head and . . .

Lynette   I was younger than you are when I first saw it.

Stephanie   I'm sorry.

Lynette   No one saw things like that back then.

Stephanie   No, I guess not.

Lynette   It was . . . over and over we watched it. So many times.

Stephanie   I don't know what to say.

Lynette   You see?

Stephanie   And they changed it? The copy?

Lynette   The commission or the FBI. I don't know, but yes, they changed it. They changed it so that everybody could get on with their lives.

Stephanie   And nobody knows you have the real thing?

Lynette   Just us.

Stephanie   God.

Lynette   So what should I do, Stephanie?

Stephanie   You're really asking me?

Lynette   That's what I'm doing.

Stephanie   I suppose you should tell people. They should know the truth.

Lynette   But people do.

Stephanie   They do?

Lynette   Deep down, they know. Books and films and exposés and witnesses, and deep down we all know. Know that something is missing. Pieces don't fit. But it's over thirty years ago. So what does it matter, really.

Stephanie   But it does matter.

Pause.

Lynette   I just wanted somebody to know.

Stephanie   Thank you. For telling me.

Lynette   I've wanted to for a long time.

Pause.

Stephanie   I have something for you, Mom.

Lynette   You do?

Stephanie   Your birthday present. It's been in my bag this whole time.

She reaches into her bag. Hands **Lynette** *a wrapped present.*

Lynette   What is it?

Stephanie   Well, open it.

Lynette   You didn't have to . . .

Stephanie   Just open it . . .

Lynette *unwraps the gift. It is a small stuffed bear.*

Lynette   It's a bear.

Stephanie   I made it myself.

Lynette   You made it?

Stephanie   Recognise the material? It's from Grandmother's coat. Her old car coat. You were throwing all her old clothes away a few years ago and I took the coat and one day I cut up the material and made this.

Lynette   It's . . . thank you, Stephanie.

Stephanie   So. Happy Birthday.

Lynette   Thank you very much.

Stephanie   I should be getting back. I'll just put the food away.

Lynette   I'll do it.

Stephanie   Just sit.

Stephanie *goes into the house.* **Lynette** *sits off to the side. After a moment the light above the back door goes on.* **Lynette** *from the 1960s enters with* **Margie**. **Lynette** *is six months pregnant.*

Lynette (*1960s*)   This is the backyard.

Margie   Oh God, it's so big.

Lynette   It is.

Margie   Nothing but trees.

Lynette   Room for a pool, even.

Margie   Really?

Lynette   We talked about it.

Margie   I love it.

Lynette   We looked at a bunch of areas, this seemed the nicest.

Margie   Sure.

Lynette   Room for a family.

Margie   You're so lucky, Lynette.

Lynette   I hope you can come out sometimes.

Margie   We'll try.

Lynette   Like for a barbecue, and in summer, if we have a pool. You and Henry come over, take a swim.

Margie   Sounds great.

Lynette   On the weekends of course.

Margie   So, what's it like?

Lynette   What do you mean?

Margie   Starting a family?

Lynette   It's . . . wonderful.

Margie   I bet.

Lynette   You'll have kids too, Margie.

Margie   Oh, probably.

Lynette   You will. Then our kids can play together.

Margie   We're still in the city.

Lynette   We'll figure it out.

Margie   Don't you miss it sometimes? The city?

Lynette   Sometimes.

Pause.

And the magazine. Coming in to the office.

Margie   You were doing so well.

Lynette   This is what I want now.

Margie   Right.

Lynette   You want another beer?

Margie   Not now.

Lynette   I haven't had a beer in . . . since I found out I was expecting.

Margie   Bet you miss it sometimes.

Lynette   Sometimes.

Margie   So who do you think is going to win?

Lynette   Win what?

Margie   The election, stupid.

Lynette   Oh, Johnson.

Margie   We got a pool going, see how many states he carries. This is funny. There's this rumour going around. Up on four. People saying Johnson knew about . . . about Kennedy being killed.

Lynette   Don't say that, Margie.

Margie   I'm only repeating what I've heard. Apparently there's some phone call, some recording of this phone call, Johnson's in on the assassination. Payback for being passed over in 1960.

Lynette   That's in really bad taste, Margie.

Margie   Some people believe it.

Lynette   Well, I don't.

Margie   It's not impossible.

Lynette   He's the President, Margie. You shouldn't talk about the President like that.

Margie   All right. It's just some talk.

Lynette   Well, change the subject.

Margie   OK.

Beat.

It's a great house.

Lynette   Yes.

Margie   And we'll still see each other, no matter what.

Lynette   We will.

Lynette *turns away.*

Margie   Hey, what is it? Lynette, what's the matter?

Lynette   I'm scared.

Margie   You're what?

Lynette   Sometimes I'm out here, all alone. Eddie's at his office and I just sit out here, for hours. I don't know anyone, I'm all alone and I get so afraid something terrible is going to happen. I thought, I move away from the city, everything would be good, things would be perfect, you know, just perfect, like I pictured it. But it's not, it's not like that at all,

the way I thought, I have no one to tell things to, I don't
know what to do, Margie, I don't know what to do here.

Margie It's OK.

Lynette There's all these things I want to talk about, but
there's no one here to talk to.

Margie Can't you talk to Eddie?

Lynette I try to . . . but we never seem to get around to
the things I want to talk about. The things that scare me. I
start to talk about them and I can see he goes away, he just
goes to a different place, so I have to hold it all inside me.

Margie You'll be fine. You're just . . . worried about
having a baby.

Lynette It's not only that.

Margie Then what?

Lynette I . . . I'm sorry.

Margie No, I'm your friend, Lynette.

Lynette What if I die? Would anyone notice?

Margie What are you talking about?

Lynette If there was an accident, would anyone ask what
happened?

Margie You're not making any sense.

Lynette I know I'm not. I'm sorry.

Margie You got to calm down. Just calm down now.

Lynette I guess I'm overexcited.

Margie That's it.

Lynette I'll be OK now.

Margie To have a beautiful house and a . . . a wonderful
husband.

Lynette Yes.

Margie You have a kid on the way and you have to think about that, about this life you're carrying. You have to be strong, Lynette.

Lynette I will.

Margie And you want to talk, any time, I'm there for you. You just call me up.

Lynette Even at work?

Margie There'll be plenty of time to . . . and we'll come out, on weekends. Swim in your new pool. And our kids, they'll play together and we'll have the best times, the best.

Lynette We will.

Margie You'll see.

Lynette The best.

Pause.

We talked about eggshell, the colour for the kitchen.

Margie That's a great colour.

Lynette Makes the room look bigger. That's what I read.

Margie I heard that.

Lynette It's getting late, I guess you should head back. I'll drive you to the train station.

Margie OK.

Lynette It was great to see you.

Margie It was really great. You feeling OK now?

Lynette Sure it's . . . having a baby – you get all confused.

Margie That's it.

Lynette I was just confused. I'm better now.

Lynette *from the 1960s and* **Margie** *go inside. After a beat*
Lynette *from the 1990s stands and takes the film from the projector.*
She walks over to the barbeque. She puts the film in the barbecue and
sets it on fire. She watches it burn.

Lynette   The President is bent forward. The right side of
his skull explodes. The President is slammed backwards and
to the left, he slides towards the floor. The First Lady climbs
towards the rear of the limousine. The car begins to
accelerate.

Lights fade.